DATE DUE

NOV - - 2002

SCIENCE PROJECT IDEAS

Science Project Ideas About

KITCHEN CHEMISTRY

Revised Edition

Robert Gardner

Enslow Publishers, Inc.

40 Industrial Road   PO Box 38
Box 398   Aldershot
Berkeley Heights, NJ 07922   Hants GU12 6BP
USA   UK

http://www.enslow.com

Library of Congress Cataloging-in-Publication Data

Gardner, Robert, 1929–.
    Science project ideas about kitchen chemistry / Robert Gardner.—Rev. ed.
        p. cm. — (Science project ideas)
    Originally published as Kitchen chemistry.
    Includes bibliographical references and index.
    ISBN 0-7660-1706-0
    1. Chemistry—Experiments—Juvenile literature. [1. Chemistry—
Experiments. 2. Experiments. 3. Science projects.] I. Title
    QD38 .G382   2002
    540'.78—dc21

                                        2001000704

Printed in the United States of America

This book was originally published in 1988 by Julian Messner as *Kitchen
Chemistry*.

10 9 8 7 6 5 4 3 2 1

To Our Readers:
We have done our best to make sure all Internet addresses in this book were
active and appropriate when we went to press. However, the author and the
publisher have no control over and assume no liability for the material available
on those Internet sites or on other Web sites they may link to. Any comments or
suggestions can be sent by e-mail to comments@enslow.com or to the address on
the back cover.

Illustration Credits: Stephen F. Delisle, pp. 63, 105; Enslow
Publishers, Inc., pp. 39, 112, 120, 123; Gary Koellhoffer, pp. 13, 14, 18, 22,
27, 44, 55, 56, 82, 94, 107, 109, 110, 114, 116, 117.

Cover Illustration: Jerry McCrea (foreground); © Corel Corporation
(background).

CONTENTS

Introduction. 4

Safety First 5

1   Chemistry in and near
    the Kitchen Sink. 6

2   Chemistry in
    the Refrigerator. 46

3   Chemistry on
    the Stove 71

4   Chemistry on
    the Kitchen Counter. 95

    Further Reading
    and Internet Addresses 126

    Index 127

INTRODUCTION

Your kitchen, in addition to being a place to prepare meals and wash dishes, is a well-equipped science laboratory. You can heat materials on the stove, cool them in the refrigerator, and submerge objects in the sink. Hot and cold water is at your fingertips; ice cubes are but a step away; the oven will keep things at a constant warm temperature, while the refrigerator and freezer can maintain constant cold temperatures. A young science enthusiast has more counter space in the family kitchen than most college students can find in their laboratories. Kitchen cabinets, pantries, and refrigerators are stocked with chemicals and other materials needed for experiments.

This book describes experiments you can do at the kitchen counter, stove, sink, or refrigerator; a few require you to move all about the kitchen. Some of these experiments take time. You may have to leave your material for several hours or days to see what happens. Be sure to leave lengthy experiments where they do not get in the way of people who have chores to do in the kitchen. Your parents will be happier about your experimentation if you do not interfere with their work and if you clean up after you finish each experiment. Thoughtful scientists do not allow their experimentation to keep others from their work. You should form the habit of working with care, especially in experiments that involve the stove or glass materials.

Most of the experiments provide a lot of guidance. But some of them will raise questions and ask you to make up your own experiments to answer them. This is the kind of experiment that could be a particularly good start for a science fair project. Such experiments are marked with an asterisk (*).

You can add to the value of the experiments you do by keeping notes on them. Set up an experiment notebook and record carefully the work you do and details like amounts and time involved. In doing some of these experiments, you may discover new questions that you can answer with experiments of your own. By all means, carry out these experiments (with your parents' or teacher's permission). You are developing the kind of curiosity that is shared by all scientists.

SAFETY FIRST

Science in the kitchen sometimes involves using things that can be dangerous, such as flames, matches, and chemicals that are poisonous. As you do the activities and experiments described in this or any other book, do them safely. Keep in mind the rules listed below and follow them faithfully.

1. Any experiments that you do should be done under the supervision of a parent, teacher, or another knowledgeable adult.

2. Read all instructions carefully. If you have questions, check with an adult. Do not take chances.

3. If you work with a friend who enjoys science too, maintain a serious attitude while experimenting. Horseplay can be dangerous to you and to others.

4. Do not taste chemicals unless instructed to do so. Many of them are poisonous.

5. Keep flammable materials such as rubbing alcohol away from flames and other sources of heat.

6. If you are using matches or flames, have a fire extinguisher nearby and know how to use it.

7. Keep the area where you are experimenting clean and organized. When you have finished, clean up and put away the materials you were using.

8. Do not touch glass that has just been heated. If you should get burned, rinse the area with cool water and notify an adult.

9. Never experiment with the electricity that comes from wall outlets unless under the close supervision of a knowledgeable adult.

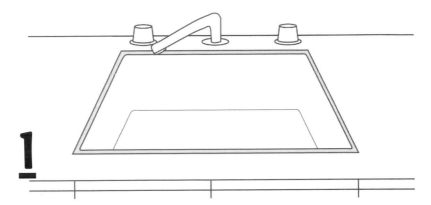

1

CHEMISTRY IN AND NEAR THE KITCHEN SINK

The most commonly used liquid in chemistry is water. It has very interesting properties of its own, and it provides a way of bringing chemicals together. What could be a more convenient place to investigate this common yet vital liquid than your own kitchen sink?

HEAPING LIQUIDS

To do this experiment you will need:

- ✔ medicine cup, test tube, or vial
- ✔ water
- ✔ eyedropper
- ✔ ruler
- ✔ sheet of dark paper
- ✔ straight pins
- ✔ drinking glass
- ✔ soapy water
- ✔ rubbing alcohol
- ✔ cooking oil

You have seen baskets with berries, apples, or other fruit heaped well above the baskets' rims. Did you know that liquids can be heaped this way too?

Fill a medicine cup, test tube, or a vial (like the small bottles that pills from a drugstore come in) level to the brim with water. Use an eyedropper to add more water to the container. You will be amazed at how high you can heap water above the rim of the cup, tube, or vial. Use a ruler to measure the height of the water. A piece of dark paper behind the heaped water will help you to see it better.

Your results should convince you that water holds together very well. It really sticks to itself.

Repeat the experiment, but this time count the number of drops you add to the brim-filled container before the water spills over the side. By counting the number of drops it takes to collect 10 ml (1 fluid oz) of water, you can figure out what volume of water you heaped above the top.

Try adding straight pins to a glass filled to the brim with water. How many pins can you add to the glass before the water spills over the rim?

Do other liquids stick together as well as water? You can find out by heaping other liquids in the same or identical containers. Try measuring the heaped heights and volumes of such liquids as soapy water, rubbing alcohol, and cooking oil. If you use the same eyedropper for all the liquids, be sure to clean and rinse it thoroughly between experiments.

Which liquid seems to stick together best?

A prediction: Try to tell ahead of time what will happen if you add a drop of soapy water to plain water heaped well above the rim of a container. Try it. Were you right?

Experiment 1.2*

DROPS OF LIQUID

To do this experiment you will need:

✔ eyedropper	✔ glass
✔ water	✔ newspaper
✔ waxed paper	✔ rubbing alcohol
✔ aluminum foil	✔ soapy water
✔ plastic wrap	✔ cooking oil

From the way different liquids heap, perhaps you can predict which liquid will form the biggest drops. It is difficult to measure the size of a single drop, but with a medicine cup and eyedropper, you can measure the volume of many drops and then divide to find the volume of just one drop.

Count the number of drops of water as you fill a medicine cup to the 10-ml line (10 ml or 10 cc). If it takes 200 drops, then each drop is 1/20 ml (10 ml/200 = 1/20 ml).

Repeat the experiment using rubbing alcohol, soapy water, and cooking oil. Which liquid forms the largest drops?

After thoroughly cleaning and rinsing the eyedropper, place a drop of plain water on a sheet of waxed paper. Look at the drop from the side. What does it look like? To see how water drops attract one another, place a second drop very close to the first one. You will see the drops "leap" together.

Drop some small puddles of water on the waxed paper. Make two-drop, three-drop, five-drop, ten-drop, and twenty-drop puddles. How do these puddles compare in shape with the single-drop puddle?

Next, prepare similar puddles using soapy water. How do these drops and puddles compare with the plain water drops and puddles?

After thoroughly washing and rinsing the eyedropper, repeat the experiment again using drops of rubbing alcohol. Then try drops of cooking oil. How do these drops and puddles compare with those made from plain and soapy water?

Does the surface on which you place a drop affect its shape? To find out, place a drop of water on waxed paper, aluminum foil, plastic wrap, glass, and newspaper. Look at these drops from the side. Does the surface the water drops are on affect their shape?

Repeat the experiment using drops of rubbing alcohol, soapy water, and cooking oil. Does the surface affect the shape of these drops?

A prediction: A liquid drop on a surface has a shape like the lens in a magnifying glass or microscope. Can you predict which liquid—water, rubbing alcohol, soapy water, or cooking oil—will magnify the most? To test your prediction, place a drop of each liquid over identical letters on some newspaper print. Which liquid makes the letter look biggest? If the liquid sinks into the paper, place a sheet of clear plastic wrap or waxed paper over the print.

Was your prediction correct?

Experiment 1.3

CLIMBING WATER

To do this experiment you will need:

- ✔ paper towel
- ✔ scissors
- ✔ water
- ✔ bowl
- ✔ food coloring
- ✔ waxed paper
- ✔ tape

The force of gravity pulls everything toward the center of the earth. That is why a stone or ball falls to the ground when you release it; it is why you always come back down no matter how high you jump. But in this experiment you will discover forces stronger than gravity— forces that cause water and other liquids to climb upward, defying the force of gravity.

To see water defy gravity, cut a 1-in-wide strip from a paper towel. Hang the paper strip so that one end is in some water, as shown in Figure 1. Add a few drops of food coloring to the water so you can watch the water move into the paper. (You may find the dyes in the coloring separating into different colors as water rises in the paper.)

Where is the liquid level in the paper strip after several hours? How high will it be tomorrow? Will it continue to rise forever?

You might like to see how water rises in other materials. You could try other brands of paper towels, different kinds of cloth, blotter paper, string, wood, and other substances.

Does water rise to different levels in different materials?

Repeat this experiment using a paper towel strip that is covered with a tube made from

FIGURE 1

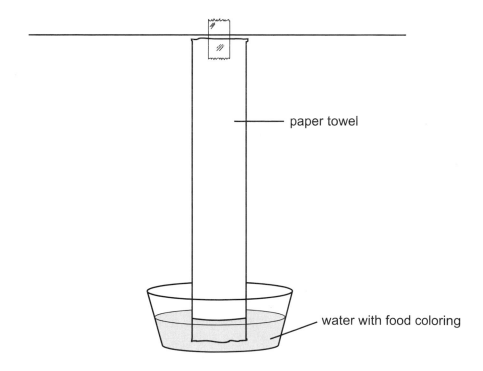

paper towel

water with food coloring

FIGURE 2

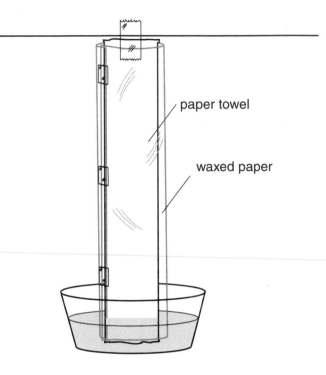

paper towel

waxed paper

waxed paper. You can seal the edges of the waxed paper with tape. (See Figure 2.) Can you explain why the water rises higher in the covered strip than it did in the one that was uncovered? If not, try the next experiment.

Experiment 1.4

Drying Wet Towels

To do this experiment you will need:

✔ paper towels   ✔ tape
✔ water   ✔ covered container

Wet two identical paper towels. Tape one so it hangs in the air. Put the other towel in a covered container. Which towel dries faster? Can you now explain why water rose higher when the paper towel strip was covered in Experiment 1.3?

But the basic question is still unanswered: How can water defy gravity in the paper strips you have tested?

Experiment 1.5*

HOW WATER DEFIES GRAVITY

To do this experiment you will need:

- ✔ paper towels
- ✔ magnifying glass or microscope
- ✔ water
- ✔ 2 clean, dry water glasses
- ✔ food coloring
- ✔ tray
- ✔ 2 flat windowpanes or glass squares
- ✔ 2 large rubber bands
- ✔ thin strip of wood or plastic
- ✔ vial
- ✔ Queen Anne's lace flower
- ✔ small drinking glasses
- ✔ soapy water
- ✔ rubbing alcohol
- ✔ cooking oil
- ✔ salt water
- ✔ waxed paper
- ✔ sink

To understand how water rises in a paper towel, you first need to see what a paper towel is made of. Tear apart a small piece of paper towel. Look at the edges of the torn paper through a magnifying glass or a microscope. You will see that the towel is made up of tiny wood fibers packed very close together. Under a good microscope, you can see water rising in the tiny spaces *between* the fibers when the towel's edge is dipped in water.

The rise of water in narrow spaces is called *capillarity*. But giving it a name does not mean we understand it. We do know that water is a very *cohesive* liquid: It sticks together well. That is why water can form such large drops. Water also adheres (sticks) to many other materials. If you turn a wet dish over, some of the water will remain stuck to the dish. The adhesion between water and glass and water and many other materials shows us that there are strong attractive forces between water and these materials.

The force of attraction between water and wood or cloth fibers causes water to move into the tiny spaces between these fibers. Because water itself is very cohesive, the water adhering to the fibers is in contact with portions of water not touching the fibers. This water is pulled upward by the cohesive forces between it and water that has adhered to the wood fibers.

You can see how water adheres to glass and how it rises higher as the spaces grow smaller by doing the following experiment. Place two clean, dry water glasses in a tray of colored water. Move the sides of the two glasses very close together and watch the water rise in the small space between the two glasses. What happens to the water level as you move the glasses closer together? Farther apart?

You can use two flat pieces of glass such as windowpanes to illustrate this effect even more clearly. (**Be careful not to cut your hands.**) Bind the glass plates together with a pair of large rubber bands. Place a thin strip of wood or plastic between the glass plates at one end to form a thin wedge of air. Put the glass plates in a tray of colored water and watch the water rise between the plates. (See Figure 3.) See if you can predict at which end of the air wedge the water will rise higher.

FIGURE 3

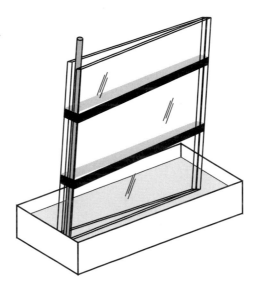

Look closely at the surface of the water in a vial. Notice that the water level is highest where the water touches the glass. The curved surface of the water is called the *meniscus*. From what you have found in these experiments, can you explain why water has a meniscus?

Using Capillarity to Color Flowers

During the summer you can probably find Queen Anne's lace blooming in a field near your home. Cut a few such flowers and bring them into your kitchen. Put one or two stalks in several small glasses of water. Add a different food coloring to the water in each glass.

Watch the white petals of these flowers over several hours. Do the food colors ascend the stalks of these flowers the way they do strips of paper towel? How can you tell?

Can you produce new colors by mixing the food colors that you add to the water in the glasses?

Carefully split the stem of a Queen Anne's lace, a white carnation, or any white flower. Place one side of the stem in water colored with red food coloring and the other in water colored by green or blue food coloring. Will you obtain a two-colored flower? Or will the colors mix to produce a third color?

Other Liquid Climbers

Will other liquids climb paper towels as well as water, or are they less defiant of gravity? To find out, place the lower ends of identical hanging strips of paper towel in soapy water, rubbing alcohol, cooking oil, salt water, and plain water. Leave the strips for several days. What do you find? Are the results different if the strips are covered with waxed paper? Does the width of the paper strip affect the height to which the water rises?

Try strips of different widths in colored water. Make some as narrow as 1/4 in; others could be 1/2 in, 1, 2, and 3 in wide. How do you explain the results?

You can make a paper-towel siphon. Just place one end of a folded paper towel in a tray of water on your kitchen counter. Let the other end of the towel hang into the sink. The towel acts like a siphon and transfers water from the tray to the sink.

Will the siphon work if you raise the end that is in the sink until it is higher than the water level in the tray?

Experiment 1.6

SEPARATING COLORS

To do this experiment you will need:

- ✔ paper towel or white blotter paper
- ✔ scissors
- ✔ watercolor paintbrush or toothpick
- ✔ food coloring
- ✔ container
- ✔ water
- ✔ tape
- ✔ black ink
- ✔ Mercurochrome

Chemists sometimes separate chemicals by a method known as *chromatography*. To see how chromatography works, cut several 1-in-wide strips from a paper towel or, better, from a sheet of white blotter paper. Using a watercolor paintbrush or a toothpick, paint a stripe of red food coloring across one of the strips about 2 in from one end. When the food coloring is dry, suspend the tip of the paper strip nearest the colored stripe in a container of water in the sink. Tape the other end to the side of the sink (see Figure 4).

Watch what happens as water carries the food coloring along the paper strip. Did the

FIGURE 4

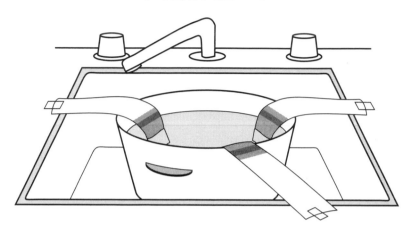

food coloring contain more than one dye? How can you tell?

Repeat the experiment using fresh strips. Paint stripes of different food coloring, black ink, Mercurochrome, and mixtures of food colorings, and ink and Mercurochrome. What do you find?

WHICH PAPER TOWEL IS BEST?

To do this experiment you will need:

✔ water	✔ large plastic bowl or dish
✔ measuring cup	✔ a friend
✔ different brands of paper towels	✔ sink

You can find many different brands of paper towels in a supermarket and see the commercials for them on television. Which brand is best?

The answer to that question depends on how you want to use the towel and how much money it is worth to you. But you can certainly test to see which towel absorbs the most water, which one absorbs water fastest, and which one is strongest.

Test 1: How Much Water Does Each Brand of Towel Absorb?

To find out, pour 230 ml (8 fluid oz) of water into a measuring cup. Take two paper towels of the same brand; fold and submerge them in the cup. When the towels are thoroughly wet, remove them from the water and let any excess water drip back into the cup. How much water is left in the cup? How much water did the towels absorb? Repeat this experiment for each brand of towel. Which brand absorbs the most water per towel?

How many towels are in each roll of each different brand? Which brand absorbs the most water per roll?

How much did each roll cost? Which brand is the best buy in terms of water absorbed per penny?

Test 2: Which Towel Absorbs Water Fastest?

Fold two paper towels from a roll and dip one end into 230 ml (8 fluid oz) of water in a measuring cup. As water flows into the towel, keep the water level in the towel even with the water level in the cup. After one minute, remove the towel and let the excess water drip back into the cup. How much water did the towels absorb in one minute?

Repeat this test for each brand of towel. Which brand absorbs water fastest?

Test 3: Which Towel Is Strongest?

Place a large plastic bowl or dish at the center of a *dry* paper towel. Have a friend hold the towel over the sink while you add measured amounts of water to the plastic bowl. Be careful not to wet the towel. How many milliliters (fluid ounces) of water can the towel support before it breaks?

Repeat the experiment using different brands. Which brand of towel is strongest when dry?

How can you find out which brand of towel is strongest when wet?

Experiment 1.8

FALLING WATER

To do this experiment you will need:

- ✔ Styrofoam cup
- ✔ pin
- ✔ small nail
- ✔ ruler
- ✔ soapy water
- ✔ stool or chair
- ✔ container
- ✔ sink

When a thin stream of water falls from a faucet, it breaks into drops. Does the size of the stream affect the point at which the water pulls itself together to form drops? You can find out by punching two holes in the bottom of a Styrofoam cup. Use a pin to punch a hole about 1.5 mm (1/16 in) in diameter in one side of the bottom of the cup. Use a small nail to punch a hole twice as wide about an inch from the smaller hole. Punch the holes from the *inside out* so you can pull away any pieces of Styrofoam around the holes that might make the streams irregular. (See Figure 5.)

Fill the cup with water and compare the distances the two streams fall before they form drops. Use a ruler to measure the length of the unbroken columns.

Does the water level in the cup affect the length of the unbroken columns? Which stream stops flowing first? Why do you think the water stops flowing from both holes before the cup is completely empty?

Fill the cup with soapy water and measure the length of the unbroken liquid columns. Because streams of soapy water are very sensitive to vibrations or movements, it would be wise to rest the cup on the edge of a stool or chair over the sink. The soapy water can be collected in a container placed in the sink so that you can repeat your measurements. Why do you think the soapy-water streams are longer than the plain-water streams of the same diameter?

FIGURE 5

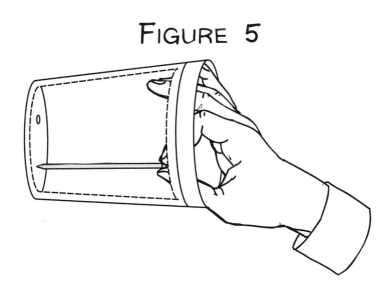

Experiment 1.9

WATER'S SKIN

To do this experiment you will need:

- ✔ container
- ✔ water
- ✔ fork or bent paper clip
- ✔ paper clip, needle, or straight pin
- ✔ liquid soap
- ✔ rubbing alcohol
- ✔ cooking oil

Water holds together so well that it behaves as if it had an invisible skin. To see this for yourself, fill a clean, well-rinsed container with water. Using a fork or a bent paper clip, gently place a paper clip, needle, or straight pin on the water's surface. Amazingly, the water surface will support the small piece of metal. Look closely! You will see that the water surface is "bent" much as the skin on your palm bends when you push it with your finger.

What happens to the floating piece of metal if you add a single drop of liquid soap to the water?

Do you think the small piece of metal can be made to float on soapy water? On rubbing alcohol? On cooking oil?

Experiment 1.10*

DISAPPEARING SOLIDS

To do this experiment you will need:

✔ sugar	✔ measuring cup
✔ teaspoon	✔ hot water
✔ 2 drinking glasses	✔ kosher salt
✔ water	

Have you ever watched colored, flavored crystals disappear in water as you stirred them while preparing a cool drink on a hot day? When a solid, such as sugar, disappears in a liquid, we say the solid, or *solute*, has dissolved in the liquid, or *solvent*, to make a *solution*.

Can you dissolve as much solid as you want in water, or is there a limit? Will solids dissolve in liquids other than water? Will liquids dissolve in other liquids? Will gases dissolve in liquids? Does temperature have any effect on the preparation of solutions? Can you dissolve two solutes in the same solvent? Can you separate solute from solvent once a solution is made? Will stirring make a solute dissolve faster?

The following experiments will enable you to answer these questions. Be sure to label and save the solutions you make so that you can use them again.

To Stir or Not to Stir?

Place 1 tsp of sugar in each of two glasses that contain the same amount of water. Use a spoon to stir the water and sugar in one glass but not the other.

Does stirring make sugar dissolve faster? Will stirring make salt dissolve faster?

Sugar in Water

Use a measuring cup to add 120 ml (4 fluid oz) of cold water to a clean drinking glass. Add a level teaspoon of sugar to the water. (You can use a card or ruler to sweep off crystals above the edge of the spoon.) Stir the water until all the sugar dissolves. How many teaspoons of sugar can you dissolve in the water? Can you taste the sugar in the water?

When no more solid can be dissolved in the solvent, we say the solution is *saturated*.

A prediction: See if you can predict how many teaspoons of sugar you will need to make a saturated solution using 240 ml (8 fluid oz) of water. Were you right?

A Hot Solution

Repeat the experiment, but this time use 120 ml (4 fluid oz) of *hot* water. How much sugar does it take to make a saturated solution when you use hot water? Does the temperature of the water change the amount of sugar that can be dissolved in 120 ml (4 fluid oz) of water?

Pour the clear, hot solution into another glass to separate it from any dissolved sugar at the bottom of the first glass. Look at the clear, hot solution every few minutes as it cools. What happens? Taste the solid that collects at the bottom of the glass. What is it? Why do you think it comes out of solution?

Salt Solutions

How much salt (sodium chloride) will dissolve in 120 ml (4 fluid oz) of cold water? (Use kosher salt if possible. Most other table salts contain additives that may make the solution cloudy.) Can you taste the salt in the water?

Try to predict how much salt will dissolve in 240 ml (8 fluid oz) of cold water. Were you right?

Do you think more salt will dissolve in 8 oz of hot water? Try it. Are you surprised by what you find?

Experiment 1.11

TWO SOLUTES IN ONE SOLVENT

To do this experiment you will need:

✔ teaspoon   ✔ water

✔ sugar   ✔ salt

✔ drinking glass

Will sugar dissolve in a saturated solution of salt and water? Add 1 tsp of sugar to a glass half full of saturated salt solution. Does the sugar dissolve?

Do you think salt will dissolve in a saturated solution of sugar and water? Try it. Were you right?

Experiment 1.12

OTHER SOLVENTS

To do this experiment you will need:

- ✔ salt
- ✔ sugar
- ✔ baking soda
- ✔ soapy water
- ✔ rubbing alcohol
- ✔ cooking oil
- ✔ vinegar
- ✔ drinking glasses
- ✔ hot water

Will salt, sugar, and baking soda dissolve in liquids other than water? Try dissolving each of the solids in soapy water, rubbing alcohol, cooking oil, and vinegar. Which solids are soluble in each liquid? What happened when you added baking soda to vinegar?

A prediction: What volume do you expect to find if you add 60 ml (2 fluid oz) of hot water to 2 fluid oz of solid sugar? Try it. Were you right? How can you explain the results of this experiment?

If you measure out equal *weights* of sugar and water and then mix them to form a solution, what do you think the total weight of the solution will be? Were you right this time?

Experiment 1.13

LIQUIDS IN LIQUIDS

To do this experiment you will need:

- ✔ cooking oil
- ✔ drinking glass
- ✔ water
- ✔ spoon
- ✔ liquid detergent

When a liquid such as rubbing alcohol dissolves in water, we say the liquids are *miscible*. Add some cooking oil to half a glass of water. Are these liquids miscible? Stir the oil and water with the spoon to break up the oil into tiny droplets. When the oil droplets are spread through the water, the mixture of liquids is called an *emulsion*. If you stop stirring, the oil droplets soon collect in a separate layer above the water.

To make a longer-lasting emulsion add a few drops of liquid detergent to the oil and water before you stir it again. Do you see why a detergent is used to remove insoluble materials from dirty clothes or dishes?

Do Gases Dissolve in Liquids or Other Gases?

To do this experiment you will need:

✔ open bottle of soda	✔ shiny metal can
✔ pan	✔ warm water
✔ hot water	✔ ice
✔ cold water	✔ spoon
✔ drinking glass	✔ clear quart or liter soda bottle

The next time you open a bottle of soda, watch closely. What do you see that makes you believe there is a gas dissolved in the liquid? From this observation what can you tell about the effect of pressure on the solubility of a gas in a liquid? Try warming an open bottle of soda by placing it in a pan of hot water. How does temperature affect the solubility of a gas in a liquid? Pour some very cold water into a glass. Place the glass in a warm place and look at the liquid again after several hours. Notice the bubbles that collect in the water. These are bubbles of air that were dissolved in the water when it was colder. Is air more soluble in hot or cold water?

Gases in Other Gases

Your television or radio weather forecaster often talks about humidity. High humidity means that a lot of water vapor is dissolved in air. To see that water is dissolved in air, half fill a shiny metal can with warm water. Add small pieces of ice to the water and stir. Continue to add ice until a fine film of water begins to form on the cold can. This water, or dew, was dissolved in the air. As the air in contact with the can cools, the solution of water in air becomes saturated. As it cools further, the extra water that cannot dissolve condenses on the cold can.

A prediction: The water that comes from the faucets in your kitchen is under pressure. If you nearly fill a clear quart or liter soda bottle with cold water, what do you expect to see rising to the top of the liquid? Were you right?

If you repeat the experiment using hot water, what will be different?

GENIE IN A BOTTLE

To do this experiment you will need:

- ✔ 2 narrow-necked bottles
- ✔ hot water
- ✔ black ink or food coloring
- ✔ cold water
- ✔ paper towel
- ✔ sink
- ✔ eyedropper
- ✔ warm water

You have heard that hot air rises. Does hot water rise too?

Find two bottles with narrow necks (soft drink bottles work well). Completely fill one bottle with hot water and enough black ink or food coloring to make the liquid look very dark. Fill the second bottle with cold water. Place a small piece of paper towel over the opening of the bottle that contains cold clear water. Then carefully turn that bottle upside down and place it on top of the bottle that contains the inky water. Why doesn't the water run out when you tip the bottle upside down?

Carefully pull the piece of paper from between the two bottles and watch the genie rise.

To see why the genie rises, fill an eyedropper with some warm water that has been colored with ink or food coloring. Place the tip of the eyedropper in some cold water as shown in Figure 6. *Slowly* squeeze some of the colored warm water into the clear cold water.

Does the warm water rise or sink in the cold water?

FIGURE 6

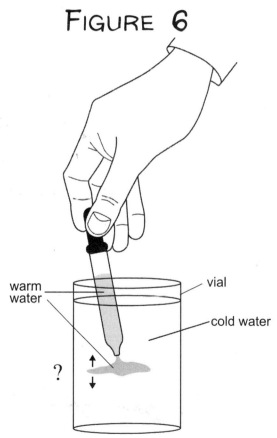

Try this experiment again, but this time squeeze a little colored cold water into some clear warm water. Does the cold liquid rise or fall in the warm water?

Would the genie rise if you used cold water in the lower bottle and hot water in the upper bottle? Try it and see.

Using food coloring and hot and cold water, see if you can prepare different colored genies. Can you make a red genie? A green one? How about a blue one?

Experiment 1.16

FIRE EXTINGUISHER GAS

To do this experiment you will need:

- ✔ birthday candle
- ✔ clay
- ✔ wide-mouthed jar
- ✔ baking soda
- ✔ vinegar
- ✔ an ADULT
- ✔ matches

You can produce the gas found in fire extinguishers by adding vinegar to baking soda. But first, place a birthday candle in a small piece of clay for support. Then cover the bottom of a wide-mouthed jar (a clean, empty peanut butter jar works well) with baking soda. Slowly pour an ounce of vinegar over the baking soda. The frothy bubbles that form are filled with carbon dioxide. Because this gas is heavier than an equal volume of air, it will soon force all the air out of the jar.

Under adult supervision, light the candle. Hold the jar above the candle and tip it so as to pour the gas (not the liquid) onto the flame. You will see the flame go out as the carbon dioxide falls over it, forcing air away from the candle.

In a carbon dioxide fire extinguisher this gas is stored in a cylinder under high pressure. When the nozzle is opened, the gas rushes out and cools as it expands. The heavy gas covers and smothers a fire.

SINKING BUBBLES, FLOATING BUBBLES

To do this experiment you will need:

- ✔ bubble-making kit
- ✔ eyedropper
- ✔ flask and one-hole stopper
- ✔ rubber tubing
- ✔ shallow dish
- ✔ seltzer tablets and water, or vinegar and baking soda
- ✔ pail or sink

If you do not have a bubble-making kit, buy one in a toy department or borrow one from a friend. After you have had some fun making air-filled bubbles and watching the beautiful colors that form, you can have some more fun making carbon dioxide bubbles. Figure 7 shows how you can do this by dipping the wide end of an eyedropper connected to a carbon dioxide generator into a dish of bubble-making liquid. Let the bubble fill with carbon dioxide gas and then gently shake the bubble off the eyedropper.

FIGURE 7

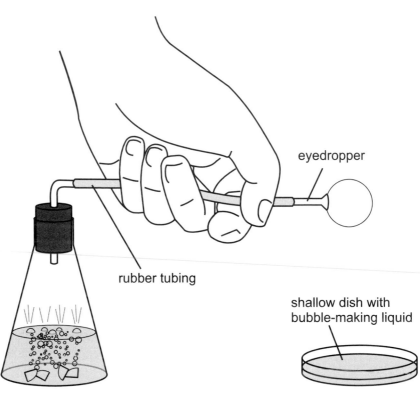

eyedropper

rubber tubing

shallow dish with
bubble-making liquid

You can make carbon dioxide by dropping seltzer tablets into water or by adding vinegar to baking soda.

Do bubbles of carbon dioxide fall faster than air-filled bubbles of the same size?

You can make air-filled bubbles float or even rise if you let them fall into a pail or sink filled with carbon dioxide. To see this, cover the bottom of a pail or sink with a thin coat of baking soda. Then add half a pint of vinegar to the powder. (Add a pint of vinegar if you use a sink.)

Let some air-filled bubbles fall into the pail or sink filled with carbon dioxide. Why do the bubbles float above the pail or sink?

2

CHEMISTRY IN THE REFRIGERATOR

Much of chemistry involves what happens when substances change from liquids to solids, or when their temperatures drop dramatically. A refrigerator enables the kitchen chemist to study such changes.

Experiment 2.1

COOLING A GAS

To do this experiment you will need:

- ✔ 2 balloons
- ✔ 2 empty 1-qt soda bottles
- ✔ freezer
- ✔ vinegar
- ✔ teaspoon
- ✔ baking soda
- ✔ 2 small pieces of paper

What happens to a gas as it cools? To find out, you can experiment with a gas that is free and plentiful—air. Attach a balloon to the neck of each of two empty 1-qt soft drink bottles. The balloons should be equally inflated, and only enough to make them stand up. Do not blow up the balloons so that they are stretched.

Put one bottle in a cold place such as a freezer. Leave the other bottle in a warm room. After an hour or so, remove the bottle from the freezer and compare the two. Which one has the bigger volume of air now? What happens to the volume of air when it cools in a closed container?

Leave both bottles in the same room for a

while. What happens to the volume of the cold gas as it warms?

Do other gases behave in the same way when they cool? You can find out by placing 30 ml (1 fluid oz) of vinegar in each of the two bottles. Then put a teaspoonful of baking soda on each of two small pieces of paper. Fold the papers over the baking soda to make two small packets. Drop one packet into each of the two quart bottles. When the reaction in a bottle is nearly complete, pull the mouth of a balloon over the neck of the bottle. What gas is in these bottles?

Put the bottles in cold and warm places as before. What happens to the volume of the carbon dioxide as it cools?

Scientists have carefully measured the volume changes as a gas cools or warms. They have found that *all* gases expand or shrink by 1/273 of their volume for each degree Celsius temperature change above or below 0°C, or 1/494 of their volume for each Fahrenheit-degree change above or below 32°F.

Experiment 2.2*

MELTING ICE

To do this experiment you will need:

- ✔ thermometer
- ✔ water
- ✔ dishpan
- ✔ ice cubes
- ✔ paper towel
- ✔ shallow bowl
- ✔ identical containers
- ✔ plastic bag
- ✔ hammer
- ✔ wide, shallow container, such as a plastic lid or plate
- ✔ ice cube tray

- ✔ pan or pail of water
- ✔ snow or crushed ice
- ✔ stirrer or spoon
- ✔ paper and pencil
- ✔ salt
- ✔ sugar
- ✔ sand
- ✔ milk
- ✔ vinegar
- ✔ short piece of thin string
- ✔ saltshaker

The freezer compartment of your refrigerator is a good place to prepare the ice and ice cubes you will need to carry out the experiments that will enable you to answer a number of questions about melting and freezing ice.

Will an Ice Cube Melt Faster in Air or in Water?

The answer could depend on the temperature of the air and water. You might guess that ice will melt faster in hot water than in cold air. Let's refine the question. Will an ice cube melt faster in air or in water if both the air and water are at the *same* temperature?

With a thermometer you can find the temperature of the air in your kitchen. By mixing hot and cold water, you can make the water temperature in a dishpan equal to the temperature of the air. When you have succeeded in doing this, place one ice cube in the water. At the same time, place an identical ice cube on a folded paper towel on the kitchen counter. Where does the ice melt faster?

Here is another experiment that will help you answer this question. Place an ice cube in some shallow water so that about half of the ice is in water and half is in air. Watch to see how the ice cube melts. What can you conclude from this experiment?

Will the Amount of Water Affect an Ice Cube's Melting Speed?

Fill identical containers with different volumes of water at the same temperature.

You might use 1/2 cup, 1 cup, 2 cups, and 4 cups of water. Add identical ice cubes to each volume of water. Does the amount of water affect the time it takes an ice cube to melt?

In which container does the water become coldest? How can you explain this?

Does the Temperature of the Water in Which the Ice Melts Affect the Ice Cube's Melting Speed?

Because you want to test the effect of temperature (not volume of water) on melting speed, you should use equal amounts of water in identical containers. You might have the water in one container at 4°C (40°F), another at 16°C (60°F), and another at 27°C (80°F), and so on.

If you used different volumes of water and different containers, you would not know whether it was the different temperatures or the different volumes or the different containers that affected the melting speed. By using equal volumes of water and identical containers, you can be sure that any differences in the melting times of the identical ice cubes that you drop into these containers will be caused by the different temperatures. A good experiment should test the effect of only one thing at a time.

How does the temperature of the water around the ice affect the melting speed? Does doubling the temperature double the speed?

Does Stirring Affect the Melting Speed of an Ice Cube?

Design an experiment to answer this question. How many containers do you need? How should the temperature and volume of water in each container compare?

Will Crushing the Ice Affect Its Melting Speed?

You can crush an ice cube by placing it in a plastic bag and tapping it with a hammer. Place the bag in a container and use the bag to line the container. Pour a pint or quart of water into the plastic-lined container and see how long it takes for the crushed ice to melt.

Pour out the water and repeat the experiment, but use an ice cube that has not been crushed. How much water should you use this time? What should its temperature be?

What do your results indicate about the effect of crushing the ice? Why do you think crushing ice affects its melting speed? The next experiment may help you to answer this question.

Does the Amount of Surface That Ice Has Affect Its Melting Speed?

The surface (the outside) of an ice cube or anything else has an area. You could measure the area of an ice cube by seeing how many 1-in or 1-cm squares you could fit on the surface of the ice. To find out if surface area affects melting speed, you can make two pieces of ice, each with a different surface area but the same volume.

To make a piece of ice with a large surface area, pour about 30 ml (1 fluid oz) of water into a wide, shallow container, such as a plastic lid or plate. You can use one section in an ice cube tray or an individual ice cube container to make a piece of ice with the same volume but a much smaller surface. When both pieces of ice are thoroughly frozen, put them in a pan or pail of water. Which piece melts faster? In which piece was more ice touching warm water?

Does the Shape of an Ice Cube Affect Its Melting Speed?

Try to figure out a way to make a cone-shaped piece of ice. How about a sphere (ball)? A cylinder?

Prepare these shapes: a regular ice cube and a flat pancake-shaped one like the one you made in the last experiment. Use the same amount of water to make each of the shapes. Which shape do you think will melt fastest? Slowest?

Place all the frozen shapes in a dishpan full of water. Was your prediction right? Which shape do you think had the largest surface area? Which one had the smallest surface area?

How Cold Can You Make Water by Adding Ice or Snow?

Place enough water in a glass or plastic container to cover the bulb of a thermometer. What is the temperature of the water? Add about 30 ml (1 fluid oz) of snow (it too is frozen water) or crushed ice and stir the ice and water mixture. What is the temperature now? Continue adding snow or crushed ice. How low does the temperature drop? Why do you think the temperature reaches a point below which it will not fall no matter how much ice or snow you add to the water?

How Cold Can You Make Water If You Put It in a Freezer?

Use a thermometer to find the temperature inside a freezer. Then place in the freezer a small container of water with a thermometer in it. The thermometer bulb should be under water as shown in Figure 8. You may find it helpful to place the container near one side of the freezer so that the freezer wall can support the thermometer. Record the temperature of the water when you begin the experiment and

FIGURE 8

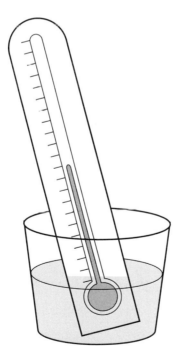

every five or ten minutes thereafter until the temperature will fall no further.

Make a graph of your readings like the one in Figure 9. What is the temperature of the water while it is freezing? How does the temperature of freezing water compare with the temperature of the ice and water mixture you examined in the previous experiment?

How cold does the ice get after it has frozen? How does the final lowest temperature of the ice compare with the temperature of the freezer that you measured at the beginning of this experiment?

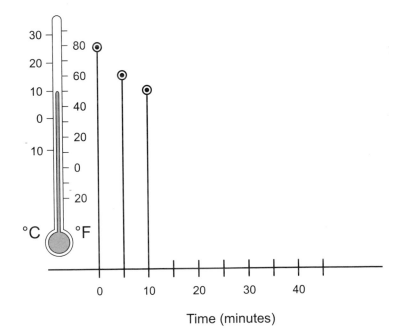

FIGURE 9

Time (minutes)

How Warm Does Ice Get Before It Melts?

In the last experiment you probably found that water freezes at about 0°C (32°F). In fact, that is how manufacturers know where to mark 0°C or 32°F on a thermometer scale.

At what temperature do you think ice will melt?

Test your prediction by removing from the freezer the container of ice with the thermometer in it that you made in the last experiment. Record the temperature of the ice as you begin and at five-minute intervals thereafter until the thermometer bulb is no longer imbedded in ice. At what temperature does ice melt? How does this temperature compare with the freezing temperature of water?

Can You Make the Temperature of Melting Ice Lower Than 0°C (32°F)?

Make a mixture of water and lots of crushed ice or snow. What is the temperature of this mix? Add 1/4 cup of salt to the ice and water mixture and stir. What is the temperature now? What happens to the temperature as you add more salt? How low can you make the temperature by adding more salt?

Now you can understand why people often put salt on icy roads or walks. What does the salt do to the freezing temperatures? Will other substances lower the freezing temperature? How about sugar? Sand? Milk? Vinegar?

Can You Lift an Ice Cube Without Touching It?

To lift an ice cube from a glass of water without touching the ice, simply lay a short piece of thin string or thread on top of the ice cube. Then sprinkle some salt from a saltshaker on the ice around the string. After a minute or two, you will be able to lift the ice cube out of the water with the string. The string will be stuck to the ice.

To see how this works, watch closely when the salt is added. The salt causes the ice around the string to melt. However, a mixture of salt and water freezes at a temperature below 0°C (32°F). The low temperature causes some of the less salty water around the string to freeze, so that it becomes stuck to the ice.

MAKING ICE CREAM

To do this experiment you will need:

- ✔ ice cream maker
- ✔ 4 cups of cream
- ✔ small pot
- ✔ stove
- ✔ an ADULT
- ✔ wooden spoon
- ✔ 1 cup sugar
- ✔ 1/8 teaspoon salt
- ✔ 1 1/2 teaspoons vanilla extract
- ✔ refrigerator
- ✔ chipped ice
- ✔ rock salt

You may know that homemade ice cream can be prepared using a mixture of salt and ice to freeze a mixture of sugar and cream. You will need to use an ice cream maker. With the old-fashioned kind of ice cream maker a crank must be turned to mix the cream and sugar, but the result is well worth the work required.

To make vanilla ice cream heat a cup of cream over low heat. (**Have an adult help you.**) Be sure the cream does not boil. Stir about 1 cup of sugar and 1/8 tsp of salt into the cream until all the solids dissolve.

Allow this mixture to cool. Then add 3 more cups of cream and 1 1/2 tsp of vanilla extract. Chill the mixture in a refrigerator.

When the creamy mixture is chilled, pour it into the container of the ice cream maker. Pack the freezing part of the ice cream maker about one-third full of chipped ice. Then add rock salt. The ratio of salt to ice should be about one to three. Continue to add ice and salt in the same ratio until the freezer is full.

Turn the cream slowly at first. When you begin to feel some resistance, turn faster. Continue turning (you may want someone to relieve you) until the creamy mixture is very stiff.

Pour off the salt water and distribute the ice cream. If you want to keep the ice cream to use as a dessert, spoon it from the mixer into a plastic container that you can place in the freezing compartment of your refrigerator.

If you continue to make ice cream, you may want to prepare different flavors using chocolate chips, fresh fruits, and various sauces. You can find ice cream recipes in many cookbooks and on the Internet.

Experiment 2.4*

SINKING ICE, FLOATING ICE

To do this experiment you will need:

- ✔ ice cubes
- ✔ glass of water
- ✔ rubbing alcohol
- ✔ cooking oil
- ✔ balance; or yardstick, pencil, string, plastic or paper plates, tall cans, and clay
- ✔ 2 small identical containers (vials, medicine cups)
- ✔ tape
- ✔ paper or paper clips
- ✔ water
- ✔ marker

Place an ice cube in a glass of water. Why do you think it floats?

If you think it is because of the tiny air bubbles in the ice, try this. Chip off a small piece of ice that has no air bubbles, or buy some clear, bubbleless ice cubes. You will find that clear ice floats in water too.

Now add an ice cube to half a glass of rubbing alcohol. Why do you think the ice sinks?

An ice cube will float in cooking oil, but just barely. It is beautiful to see because the melting ice forms giant drops of water that fall ever so slowly through the clear, thick oil. It is like watching raindrops falling in slow motion.

Perhaps ice is heavier than rubbing alcohol but lighter than water and cooking oil, but before testing this idea, we'd better decide what "heaviness" means. Certainly, an ice cube weighs more than a drop of water, and the weight of a pint of rubbing alcohol exceeds the weight of a thimbleful of water. When people say oil is lighter than water, they usually mean that a certain volume of oil weighs less than an equal volume of water. If a cup of water weighs 1/2 lb, they would predict that a cup of oil would weigh less than 1/2 lb.

You can test this idea by comparing the weights of equal volumes of water, rubbing alcohol, cooking oil, and ice. If you do not have a balance or scale, you can make a fairly sensitive balance with a yardstick, a pencil, string, and plastic or paper plates, as shown in Figure 10.

You can make a support for the fulcrum pencil (the one at the 18-inch line) from wood, or you can simply let the ends of the pencil rest on a pair of tall cans. Add clay to the yardstick, if needed, to balance the scale.

You will need two small identical containers, such as vials or plastic medicine cups, to

FIGURE 10

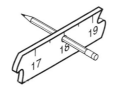

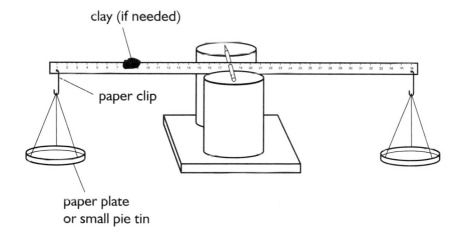

clay (if needed)

paper clip

paper plate
or small pie tin

measure out equal volumes of ice, water, rubbing alcohol, and cooking oil. If the two containers do not have quite the same weight, you can make their weights equal by taping paper or paper clips to the lighter one.

Pour water into one container until it is about three-quarters full. Mark the water level with a marking pen or a piece of tape before you put the container into the freezer.

When the water is thoroughly frozen, remove it from the freezer and note where the top of the ice is compared with the original water level. What happened to the volume as the water froze?

Place the second container next to the container of ice. Add water to the empty container until you have equal volumes of ice and water. Put the two containers on the pans at opposite ends of the balance. Which is heavier, ice or water?

In the same way, compare equal volumes of ice and rubbing alcohol, rubbing alcohol and water, and water and cooking oil. Which substance is heaviest? Which is lightest?

Do your measurements of heaviness for the same volume help you to explain why ice floats in water but sinks in rubbing alcohol?

What do you predict will happen if you pour cooking oil into rubbing alcohol? Try it. Were you right?

Experiment 2.5*

KEEPING ICE

To do this experiment you will need:

✔ ice cubes	✔ various insulating materials, such as a Styrofoam cup, newspaper, sponges, glass wool, or thermos bottle and string

It is easy to keep ice in a freezer where the temperature is below 0°C (32°F), but how did people keep ice before electric or gas freezers were invented? Even during the first third of the twentieth century, many people had iceboxes. An iceman would deliver a large cake of ice weighing 20 to 100 lb and place it in an insulated icebox. People stored food in the icebox just as they store it in a refrigerator today.

The iceman owned an icehouse where he stored the large chunks of ice he cut from frozen lakes and ponds in the winter. To keep the ice through the hot months of summer, he covered it with thick layers of sawdust. The sawdust insulated the ice even from the humid heat of July and August. The icehouse had no windows to let in warm sunlight, and it had a high roof where warm air could collect and flow through vents to the outside.

We still use insulation methods, though usually not sawdust, to prevent heat from escaping from our homes in the winter or to keep heat from entering them in the summer.

You can learn a lot about insulation by building ice-cube keepers. If heat cannot get to an ice cube easily, then the cube will melt slowly. You know how long it takes an ice cube to melt in air. Now, see how long you can keep it from melting in different insulated containers.

You might put the ice cube in a Styrofoam cup wrapped in newspaper. Or you might wrap it in sponges surrounded by glass wool. You could suspend the ice cubes on a string in a thermos bottle.

Try these and other ways to keep an ice cube. Keep trying to improve your ice keeper.

You might even like to sponsor an ice-cube-keeping contest with your classmates, your scout troop, or a club to which you belong. See who can keep an ice cube from melting the longest.

THE HEAT TO MELT ICE

To do this experiment you will need:

✔ water	✔ ice cubes
✔ 2 identical containers	✔ pitcher
✔ freezer	✔ thermometer

From the experiments you have done, you know that it takes a long time for ice to melt or water to freeze. You also know that while water is freezing or ice is melting, the temperature stays at 0°C (32°F). After all the water has frozen, the temperature of the ice falls to the temperature of the freezer. After all the ice has melted, the temperature of the water rises to that of its surroundings.

When you heat most substances, their temperature rises, but the temperature of melting ice remains at 0°C (32°F) throughout the melting process. Does this mean that no heat is needed to make ice melt? That does not seem right, does it? Certainly, ice melts faster when you hold it in your hands. You can feel your hands become colder as heat flows from your body to the ice.

In the 1700s a Scottish chemist named Joseph Black designed an experiment to find out how much heat was required to melt a certain weight of ice. You can do an experiment that is very much like the one he did.

Pour 1 cup of water into one of two identical containers. Put the water into the freezer and leave it overnight so that it will be completely frozen when you start the experiment.

When you are ready to begin, mix some ice cubes and cold water in a pitcher to obtain ice water at 0°C (32°F). Remove the container of ice from the freezer and place it on a counter near the second container. When you see that the surface of the ice is beginning to melt, you will know that the ice temperature has risen to 0°C (32°F)—the temperature of the ice water in the pitcher. Pour 1 cup of ice water into the empty container beside the ice. Record the time, and place a thermometer in the ice water.

Watch the temperature of the ice water as it warms. How long does it take the ice water to warm to 4°C (40°F)?

How long does it take the ice to melt and warm up to 4°C (40°F)?

Can you figure out a way to determine the amount of heat needed to melt ice from the information you have collected? Can you figure out how many times as much heat is needed to melt ice as to warm an equal weight of ice water through 4°C (8°F)?

Now, compare your results with Joseph Black's. He assumed that since the ice and the ice water were in the same room, the same amount of heat would flow into both during the same time. In his experiment, it took ten and one-half hours for the ice to reach the temperature (4°C) attained by the ice water in one-half hour. Black reasoned that ten additional hours were needed for the ice to reach 4°C because of the extra heat needed to melt the ice. Therefore, he believed that it took twenty times as much heat to melt a pound of ice as it did to raise the temperature of a pound of water from 0°C to 4°C. (It took the ice ten hours to melt and one-half hour to warm up to 4°C after it became water.)

One way to measure heat is in Btus (British thermal units). One Btu is the amount of heat needed to raise the temperature of 1 lb of water through 1 degree Fahrenheit. To raise the 1/2 lb of water in a cup of water through 8°F (from 32°F to 40°F) would require 4 Btus (1/2 pound x 8°F = 4 Btus). From his data, Joseph

Black would have found that it takes 160 Btus to melt 1 lb of ice (20 x 4 Btus = 80 Btus for 1/2 pound or 160 Btus for 1 pound). More accurate experiments show that it takes 144 Btus to melt 1 lb of ice. From your own results, how much heat, in Btus, do you find is needed to melt 1 lb of ice?

You can measure heat in calories as well. A calorie is the amount of heat needed to raise the temperature of 1 gram of water through 1 degree Celsius. How much heat, in calories, is needed to melt 1 gram of ice?

3

CHEMISTRY ON THE STOVE

Many chemical reactions occur only when substances are heated. Some of these reactions take place when we cook food, so it is fitting that as a kitchen chemist you use a stove for many experiments. **Be sure you have a parent's supervision when you use the stove. Stay alert to the dangers of fire. Use a pot holder to protect your hands when you touch a pan that has been heated.**

Experiment 3.1

THE HEAT TO BOIL WATER

To do this experiment you will need:

- ✔ pint of water
- ✔ thermometer
- ✔ pencil and paper
- ✔ saucepan
- ✔ stove
- ✔ an ADULT
- ✔ watch
- ✔ pot holder

In Chapter 2 you found that it takes 144 Btus of heat to melt 1 lb of ice. How much heat do you think it will take to boil away 1 lb of water?

Again, it was Joseph Black who first investigated this topic thoroughly. His method is one that you can try on the kitchen stove.

Measure the temperature of a pint of water, write down the temperature, and pour the water into a saucepan. **Under adult supervision**, place the pan on one of the burners of your kitchen stove. Turn on the heat and record the time. How long does it take to bring the water to a boil? When the water is boiling, the temperature is about 100°C (212°F) unless you live at an altitude well above sea level.

How long does it take to boil away all the liquid once the water has reached the boiling temperature? **Use the pot holder to remove the saucepan and turn off the stove *as soon as* the saucepan is empty.**

When Joseph Black did this experiment, he found that it took five minutes to warm the water from 10°C (50°F) to its boiling point. Another thirty minutes passed before all the water had changed to a gas (steam). He assumed the stove delivered the same amount of heat per minute to the water throughout the experiment. Thus, he found that it took six times as much heat to change the liquid water to gaseous water as it did to warm the water through 162°F (from 50°F to 212°F).

Had he used Btus to measure heat, Joseph Black would have found that it took 162 Btus to warm the pint of water from 50°F to the boiling point. A pint of water weighs 1 lb. A Btu, you will remember, is the amount of heat needed to warm 1 lb of water through one degree Fahrenheit. To boil away 1 lb of water would have required six times as much heat, or 972 Btus.

How do your results compare with those of Joseph Black?

How does the heat needed to change a pound of water to steam compare with the heat needed to convert a pound of ice to water?

Experiment 3.2*

HOT GAS, COLD GAS

To do this experiment you will need:

- ✔ balloons
- ✔ two 1-qt glass soda bottles
- ✔ saucepan
- ✔ water
- ✔ an ADULT
- ✔ stove

From Experiment 2.1, you know that a gas shrinks when it cools. What do you think will happen to the volume of a gas when it is heated?

Put an empty balloon over the mouth of each of two 1-qt soft drink glass bottles. Leave one bottle at room temperature so you can compare it with a second bottle that is heated in a saucepan half filled with water. **With an adult present**, heat the pan on the stove until the water begins to boil. As soon as the water is boiling, turn off the heat. What happens to a volume of air when it is heated?

Does carbon dioxide gas behave the same way? How can you find out?

Experiment 3.3*

COIN CLATTER

To do this experiment you will need:

✔ empty soda bottle	✔ refrigerator
✔ cold water	✔ coin

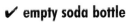

You can hear as well as see an effect produced by air as it warms. Rinse an empty soda bottle with very cold water or leave the bottle in a refrigerator for a few minutes. After the air in the bottle has been cooled, use your finger to spread some water over the lip of the bottle's opening. Then place a coin that will cover the opening on the thin film of water. As the gas in the bottle warms, you will hear and see the coin click up and down.

What causes the coin to lift? How long will this clicking go on? Will the clicking rate increase if you put the bottle in bright sunlight? Will it increase if you place it in a pan of warm water?

Experiment 3.4

CRUSHING A CAN WITH AIR PRESSURE

To do this experiment you will need:

✔ 1-gal metal can with screw-on cap or rubber stopper	✔ an ADULT
	✔ stove
✔ measuring cup	✔ gloves or pot holder
✔ water	✔ thick piece of cardboard or other heatproof mat

Many people can tell you that the pressure exerted by air at sea level is 14.7 pounds per square inch, but they do not realize the huge forces that can result from such a pressure. The total inward force on a cube one foot on each side is over *six tons*. Such a cube does not normally collapse because the air inside the cube exerts the same pressure as the air on the outside.

In this experiment, you will see what happens when we get rid of the air that is normally inside a container. Then you will be able to see the effect of the force that air pressure exerts when there is no opposing force.

You will need a 1-gal metal can, such as the kind that olive oil comes in. If the can's screw-on cap is missing, you can use a rubber stopper that fits the opening in the can.

Rinse the can very thoroughly to remove any oil that might still remain. Pour 1 cup of water into the can. Leave the top of the can open, and **with an adult to help you**, place the can on a stove. When you heat the can, the steam produced as the water boils will replace the air that was inside the container. Let the water boil for several minutes to be sure that most of the air in the can has been replaced by steam.

Using gloves or a pot holder to protect your hands, remove the can from the heat and place it on a thick piece of cardboard or some other heatproof mat. *Immediately* seal the can with its screw-on cap or a rubber stopper.

Soon, as the can cools, the steam will condense, leaving the can nearly empty. Watch the air, unopposed now by air inside the can, push inward on all sides of the can. You will be amazed how powerful air can be!

Experiment 3.5

A SUPERSATURATED SOLUTION

To do this experiment you will need:

- ✔ hypo (sodium thiosulfate) crystals
- ✔ small juice glass or test tube
- ✔ pan
- ✔ water
- ✔ an ADULT
- ✔ stove
- ✔ spoon or straw
- ✔ gloves or pot holder
- ✔ magnifying glass, optional

A saturated solution has dissolved in it all the solute it can hold at a particular temperature. But sometimes more solute can be dissolved than would normally be found in a saturated solution. Such a solution is *supersaturated*, and you can make one quite easily.

Buy some hypo (sodium thiosulfate) crystals from a photography shop, or ask your science teacher if you may use some from the school's laboratory.

Fill a small juice glass or test tube about one-quarter full with hypo crystals. Place the glass or test tube in a small pan of water, and

with an adult to help you, heat the pan on the stove until the solid turns into a liquid. There is enough water in the hypo crystals to dissolve the solid at temperatures close to 90°C (200°F). When all the solid has dissolved, stir the hypo solution with a spoon or straw and turn off the stove.

Use a glove or pot holder to remove the glass or test tube. Let the solution cool to room temperature. Since hypo is more soluble in hot water than in cold water, you may have a saturated solution after it has cooled down to room temperature.

To see if the solution is supersaturated, add a *tiny* crystal of hypo to the solution. What happens? How do you know that the solution was supersaturated?

If you have a magnifying glass, you will enjoy seeing the crystals grow around the tiny "seed" crystal. It is a beautiful sight.

Experiment 3.6

GROWING CRYSTALS

To do this experiment you will need:

- ✔ teaspoon
- ✔ potassium alum
- ✔ water
- ✔ drinking glass
- ✔ saucepan
- ✔ an ADULT

- ✔ gloves or pot holder
- ✔ 2 Styrofoam cups
- ✔ paper clip
- ✔ thread
- ✔ clean container

Crystals will emerge from a saturated solution only if we cool or evaporate water from the solution. If the water in such a solution evaporates slowly in the presence of a seed crystal, it is possible to grow large, beautiful crystals.

To prepare a saturated solution of potassium alum, begin by adding 1/2 tsp of the solid to 1/4 glass of water. (You can obtain alum from your school or pharmacy.) Stir until all the solid dissolves. Continue to add alum a half teaspoon at a time until no more solid will dissolve even after thorough stirring. How do you know this solution is saturated?

Put the glass of solution into some water in a saucepan. **Under adult supervision**, heat the saucepan until the water boils. Do you think the solution in the glass is still saturated?

To find out, see if you can dissolve another 1/2 tsp of alum in the warm solution. Add 3 more teaspoons and see if you can stir this additional solid into solution.

Turn off the heat and, **using a glove or pot holder to protect your hand**, remove the glass of hot solution from the saucepan. Pour the solution into a Styrofoam cup so that it will cool slowly. Suspend a paper clip from the center of a length of thread and hang it in the Styrofoam cup, as shown in Figure 11. A second cup, from which you have cut away the upper third, can be used to hold the thread firmly against the cup that contains the hot solution.

Leave the solution to cool for a day. When you return, you should find tiny alum crystals on the thread. Why would you expect crystals to form as this solution cools?

If there are no crystals, gently swirl the liquid in the cup. This disturbance of the supersaturated solution should cause crystals to begin forming on the thread within a few minutes.

FIGURE 11

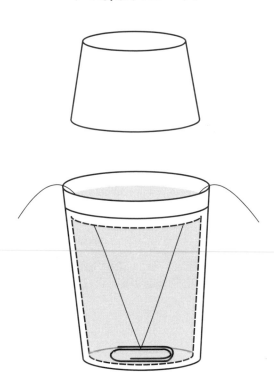

Remove the thread and paper clip from the solution. Pour the solution, but none of the crystals that may be on the bottom of the cup, into another clean container. Pull away all but one of the crystals on the thread. Tie the thread to a paper clip that has been straightened out and placed across the top of the cup. The crystal should hang in the middle of the solution. Watch it grow as the solution slowly evaporates.

Experiment 3.7

CARBON DIOXIDE AND BAKING

To do this experiment you will need:

- ✔ flour
- ✔ warm water
- ✔ baking powder
- ✔ 2 greased cake pans
- ✔ an ADULT
- ✔ stove
- ✔ empty, clean peanut butter jar
- ✔ hot tap water
- ✔ birthday candle
- ✔ matches

Carbon dioxide is a baker's friend. To see why, make two small cakes. Make the first cake by mixing flour and warm water until you have a smooth dough. Prepare the second cake by mixing three parts flour with one part baking powder. Then add warm water.

Put each cake in a small greased pan and **ask an adult to help you** heat the pan in the kitchen stove. When you think the cakes are done, turn off the heat and let them cool.

How do the two cakes compare? Break open both cakes. In which cake was carbon dioxide produced? How can you tell? Where do you think the carbon dioxide gas came from?

To see that baking powder is a source of carbon dioxide, cover the bottom of an empty, clean, pint-sized peanut butter jar with baking powder. Add some hot tap water to the jar and watch the bubbles of carbon dioxide form in the solution.

To see that the bubbles are carbon dioxide, pour the gas from the jar onto a burning birthday candle as you did in Experiment 1.16. What evidence do you have that the gas is carbon dioxide?

Experiment 3.8

INVISIBLE INK

To do this experiment you will need:

- ✔ lemon juice
- ✔ cup
- ✔ toothpick or watercolor paintbrush
- ✔ file card
- ✔ an ADULT
- ✔ large pan of water
- ✔ stove
- ✔ kitchen tongs

One type of invisible ink used by detectives in mystery stories can be prepared by a kitchen chemist. The secret ingredient is lemon juice. Just squeeze a little into a cup. Dip a toothpick or watercolor paintbrush into the lemon juice and write a message on a file card.

When the lemon-juice ink dries, it leaves a thin deposit of fine white crystals. These crystals are mostly citric acid, a solid found in lemons and other citrus fruits. The fine crystals are very difficult to see, but when the citric acid is heated, it changes to carbon (a black element) and other colored substances. So you can make the writing on the card visible by heating it. **Before you heat the**

card, ask an adult to help you. Also, place a large pan of water near or on the stove. Should the card accidentally catch fire, you can plunge it into the water.

When the "ink" is dry, hold the card with kitchen tongs and carefully move it back and forth above the heating element or burner on the kitchen stove. Keep it high enough above the flame or coil so that it does not char or burn. If it begins to scorch, raise it higher above the heat. The invisible message you wrote can now be read easily.

Experiment 3.9

MAKING THE VISIBLE INVISIBLE

To do this experiment you will need:

✔ an ADULT	✔ liquid bleach
✔ facial tissue	✔ stove

The message that you made visible by heating can be made invisible again by some more kitchen chemistry. Under adult supervision, dip a folded facial tissue into some liquid bleach and blot (don't rub) the writing gently with the damp tissue. Watch the visible become invisible again!

Liquid bleach is poisonous. Keep it away from your eyes, nose, and mouth. Wash your hands thoroughly after you finish blotting away the message.

Bleaches contain a chemical that will react with many colored substances to form colorless substances. Sometimes these colorless materials can be changed back to their colored form by heating.

Can you make the message reappear by heating the card again? Or has the invisible ink been permanently removed by the bleach? **Ask an adult** to help you heat the card. Take all the precautions you took the first time you heated the card.

Experiment 3.10*

MAKING REAL INK DISAPPEAR

To do this experiment you will need:

- ✔ black ink
- ✔ water
- ✔ drinking glass
- ✔ spoon
- ✔ an ADULT
- ✔ liquid bleach
- ✔ facial tissue
- ✔ felt-tip pen
- ✔ ballpoint pen

Can the same bleach you used in Experiment 3.9 make a dark, inky solution turn clear? Can it make a message written in normal visible ink disappear?

Add a drop or two of black ink to some water in a glass and stir to mix. **Under adult supervision**, add a few drops of liquid bleach to the dark mixture. (**Remember that the bleach is poisonous! Handle with care.**) Stir for a minute or two, and the liquid will turn clear if you have added enough bleach.

How many drops of bleach are required to clear up one drop of ink in water?

Can the same bleach on a facial tissue be used to blot away a letter written with a felt-tip pen? Can it be used to blot away a letter written with a ballpoint pen?

Be sure to wash and rinse your hands and all glassware used in this experiment.

A prediction: See if you can predict how many drops of bleach will be needed to clear up two drops of ink in water.

Were you right?

Can you predict how many drops will be needed to clear up three drops of ink in water? To clear up four drops of ink?

Experiment 3.11

MORE INVISIBLE "INK"

To do this experiment you will need:

- ✔ small sheet of paper
- ✔ pan of water
- ✔ hard, smooth surface
- ✔ dry piece of paper
- ✔ ballpoint pen

Here is a method for writing with invisible ink that is used to make the watermarks for identifying postage stamps. Dip a small sheet of paper into a pan of water. Place the wet paper on a hard, smooth surface such as a kitchen counter. Put a dry piece of paper on top of the wet one and write a message on the dry paper with a ballpoint pen. Bear down hard as you write so that the wet paper fibers underneath are crushed by the pressure you apply.

Separate the two sheets of paper and put the wet sheet aside. When it has dried, the message you wrote will be very hard to see. If you wet the paper and hold it so that it reflects light, the words can be easily seen. The smoothed, crushed fibers under the message you wrote reflect light better than the rest of the paper when wet.

A Salty Hidden Message

To do this experiment you will need:

- ✔ salt
- ✔ warm water
- ✔ drinking glass
- ✔ toothpick
- ✔ sheet of paper
- ✔ soft pencil

Prepare a small amount of salt solution using salt and warm water. Dissolve as much salt as you can. Dip the broad end of a toothpick into the salt solution and use it as a pen to write a message on a sheet of paper. Dip your "pen" into the salty "ink" often to be sure plenty of salt gets onto the paper.

After the liquid has thoroughly dried, the message remains invisible. To read what was written you can gently rub the paper with the side of the soft graphite in a pencil. Rub in different directions. You will hear a scratchy sound when you are moving the pencil in the right direction over the salt in a particular letter.

Experiment 3.13

DISAPPEARING GLASS

To do this experiment you will need:

- ✔ plain, clear drinking glass or plastic cylinder
- ✔ water
- ✔ pencil
- ✔ coin
- ✔ teacup
- ✔ Pyrex glass tubing
- ✔ cooking oil

When light passes from air to water, glass, diamond, or any other transparent material, it is bent. You can see this for yourself. Fill a plain, clear drinking glass or plastic cylinder with water. Put a pencil into the glass and look at the pencil from the side. You will see that the pencil appears to be broken at the point where it enters the water. Light passing from the pencil through the water is bent when it emerges into air.

Another way to see this effect is to place a coin on the bottom of a teacup as shown in Figure 12. Lower your head so that the coin just disappears from your view. Ask someone to slowly pour some water into the cup. The coin will become visible again.

FIGURE 12

If two substances bend light coming from air through the same angle, one will become invisible if placed in the other. Because the two substances behave in the same way with respect to light, light passing from one to the other will not be bent or reflected. Therefore, if one object is placed inside the other, light goes right through the one inside without being affected in any way.

Cooking oil and Pyrex glass bend light coming from air through the same angle. Consequently, Pyrex glass will disappear if placed in cooking oil. If possible, borrow a few short lengths of Pyrex glass tubing from your school. Place the short lengths of tubing in a clear glass of cooking oil. You will see the tubing slowly disappear as the air in the tubes becomes filled with cooking oil.

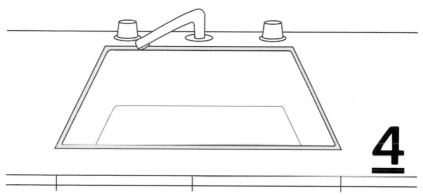

CHEMISTRY ON THE KITCHEN COUNTER

One thing that every experimental scientist needs is space to conduct research. Almost every kitchen has a counter or a table where experiments can be carried out. The experiments in this chapter do not require heat or ice. You can do them on a counter or table, but you will need water, some chemicals, and other materials that may be stored in cabinets about the kitchen and elsewhere.

Experiment 4.1*

IODINE TO INK— A TEST FOR STARCH

To do this experiment you will need:

- ✔ tincture of iodine
- ✔ eyedropper
- ✔ an ADULT
- ✔ water
- ✔ 2 drinking glasses
- ✔ teaspoon
- ✔ cornstarch
- ✔ bread, cake, and raw potato
- ✔ sugar, flour, baking soda, and salt
- ✔ medicine cups or small aluminum pans

One test that chemists and biologists use to determine the presence of starch is to add an iodine solution to a solid or liquid that is suspected to contain starch.

To see what happens when starch and iodine react, you will need to prepare an iodine solution. You can do this by adding about twenty drops of tincture of iodine to a glass of water. **Iodine is *poisonous* so do this experiment under adult supervision. Keep the iodine away from your mouth and be sure to thoroughly wash your**

hands and all glassware and utensils when you finish this experiment.

Now that you have a solution of iodine, pour about half of it into a glass with about 1/2 tsp of cornstarch. Stir the mixture. The dark blue color tells you that starch is present.

To see if some foods contain starch, add a few drops of the iodine solution to small pieces of bread, cake, and raw potato. Try adding drops of the iodine solution to some powders in medicine cups or small aluminum pans. You might test sugar, flour, baking soda, and salt in addition to cornstarch. Which of these substances contain starch? Throw away all food immediately after completing this experiment.

Experiment 4.2*

ACIDS AND BASES

To do this experiment you will need:

- ✔ an ADULT
- ✔ household ammonia
- ✔ glass or medicine cup
- ✔ litmus paper or unsweetened grape juice
- ✔ vinegar
- ✔ eyedropper
- ✔ water
- ✔ lemon juice
- ✔ orange juice
- ✔ scouring powder
- ✔ baking soda
- ✔ strong soap solution
- ✔ soda water
- ✔ tea
- ✔ aspirin

Chemists divide substances into groups. There are solids, liquids, and gases; there are mixtures and pure substances; there are elements and compounds; and there are acids, bases, and neutral substances.

Acids contain hydrogen, have a sour taste, react with metals such as zinc to form hydrogen gas, react with bases to produce salts and water, and conduct electricity when they dissolve in water.

Bases have a bitter taste, react with acids to form salt and water, and conduct electricity when they dissolve in water.

A substance such as water that appears to be neither an acid nor a base is said to be neutral.

Both acids and bases change the color of certain chemicals called indicators. For example, litmus, a purple material obtained from lichens, turns red in acids and blue in basic solutions.

To see how indicators help you identify acids and bases, you can use litmus paper if you have any at home or in school. If not, you can use unsweetened grape juice as an indicator. Grape juice is red in an acid, but turns green in a basic solution. **You will need household ammonia for this experiment. Use it under adult supervision and wash your hands afterward.**

Place a few drops of household ammonia in a glass or a medicine cup. Dip a piece of red litmus paper into the ammonia or add a drop of grape juice. Is ammonia an acid or a base?

A prediction: What do you think will happen if you hold a piece of moist red litmus paper *over* the ammonia solution?

Place a few drops of vinegar in a glass or medicine cup, and again test with litmus paper or a drop of grape juice. Is vinegar an acid or a base?

Vinegar is a dilute solution of acetic acid. Can it be neutralized by the basic ammonia solution?

To find out, add ammonia drop by drop to the vinegar until the red litmus turns blue, or until drops of the grape juice turn green.

See if you can predict how many ounces of vinegar you will need to neutralize an ounce of the household ammonia you used before. To neutralize the ammonia means to remove its basic properties by allowing it to react with acid until it has changed to salt and water.

Add a few drops of grape juice to 30 ml (1 fluid oz) of ammonia. Then pour measured volumes of vinegar into the ammonia solution until the color quickly changes from green to red.

Did you predict the volume needed correctly?

Using grape juice or litmus paper as an indicator, find out if the following are acidic, basic, or neutral: water, lemon juice, orange juice, a solution of scouring powder, baking soda in water, a strong soap solution, soda water, tea, and aspirin in water.

Add a few drops of grape juice to an ounce of vinegar in a glass. Can you neutralize the acidic vinegar by adding baking soda?

A prediction: Add about 15 ml (1/2 fluid oz) of grape juice to 150 ml (5 fluid oz) of water in a glass. If the mixture is not green, add ammonia drop by drop until it turns green. What do you predict will happen if you add a seltzer tablet to the green solution?

Experiment 4.3*

BOUNCING BUTTONS

To do this experiment you will need:

✔ ginger ale or club soda	✔ vinegar
✔ clear glass	✔ seltzer tablets
✔ small button	✔ raisins
✔ baking soda	✔ plastic knife

In the last experiment, you saw bubbles of gas forming when you added baking soda (sodium bicarbonate) to vinegar. These same bubbles of carbon dioxide gas are found in carbonated beverages such as cola, ginger ale, and club soda. The bubbles can be used to lift a button.

Pour some ginger ale or club soda from a freshly opened bottle into a clear glass. Drop a small button into the liquid. It will sink, but it will soon rise to the surface, rest for a few seconds, and then sink once more.

As long as there are carbon dioxide bubbles in the liquid, the button will continue to bounce up and down in the glass. If the bouncing button begins to lose its tempo, simply add a little more ginger ale to the glass.

To see why the button bounces as it does, watch closely as it settles on the bottom. Notice that the gas bubbles stick to the sunken button. As bubbles collect on the button, they make the combination of bubbles and button lighter than an equal volume of water. As a result, the button with its attached bubbles rise to the surface.

Watch the button as it rests on the surface. Why does it sink again?

See if you can make the button bounce using baking soda and vinegar. Will the button bounce if the carbon dioxide bubbles come from seltzer tablets?

Dancing Raisins

Buttons are not the only things that will bounce about in carbonated beverages. Pieces of raisins will "dance" nicely in a glass of cola or soda water.

To see the dance of the raisins, cut several raisins into quarters with a plastic knife, and add them to a freshly poured glass of ginger ale or club soda.

Look closely. Can you find tiny gas bubbles clinging to the raisins? Why do you think the raisins do their peculiar dance in the liquid? Would they dance in a glass of water? In a glass of hot water fresh from the faucet?

Experiment 4.4

A LEAPING FLAME

To do this experiment you will need:

- ✔ an ADULT
- ✔ matches
- ✔ candle
- ✔ candle holder

To see a flame leap, you are going to have to use matches. **Because matches are dangerous, have a parent or other adult help you with this experiment.** The adult will enjoy the experiment as much as you will.

Place a candle in a holder or on a metal lid and light it. After the candle has burned for several minutes, light another match and blow out the candle. Bring the match to the stream of white smoke that rises from the extinguished candle. (See Figure 13.) You will find that the flame will follow the smoke stream back to the wick and ignite the candle again. The flame seems to leap from the match down to the wick.

Repeat this experiment several times. How far can you get the flame to jump?

FIGURE 13

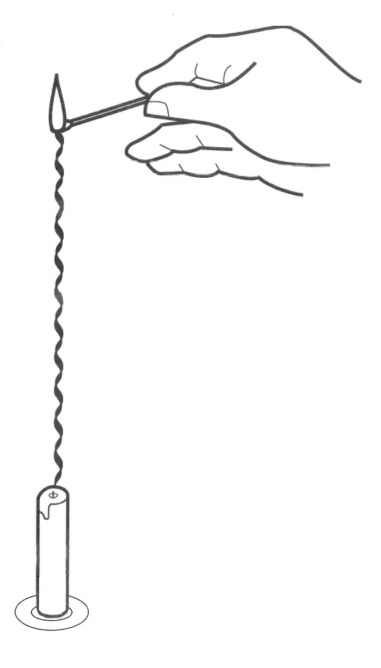

Experiment 4.5*

A BURNING CANDLE

To do this experiment you will need:

- ✔ an ADULT
- ✔ matches
- ✔ used short candle
- ✔ glass
- ✔ water
- ✔ candle

- ✔ magnifying glass
- ✔ wooden toothpicks
- ✔ straight pin
- ✔ eyedropper
- ✔ aluminum foil

In this investigation of what makes a candle burn, you will again be using matches. **Have a parent or other adult help you with these experiments.**

Light a candle that has been used and is not very tall. Watch it burn. How many colors do you see in the flame? What is the shape of the flame? Where does the flame begin and end?

You cannot get inside the flame to see that there is no burning there, but you can do an experiment that will show you that burning occurs along the outside of the flame.

Hold a glass partly filled with water well above the flame. When the flame is burning steadily and evenly, lower the bottom of the glass into the flame's center for about one second. (See Figure 14.) Lift the glass out of the flame and you will see a ring of soot where the flame was burning.

Look closely at the wick of a candle that is not burning. Use a magnifying glass if you have one. You can see that the wick is made up of threads woven together. Melted candle wax will move up the spaces between these threads

FIGURE 14

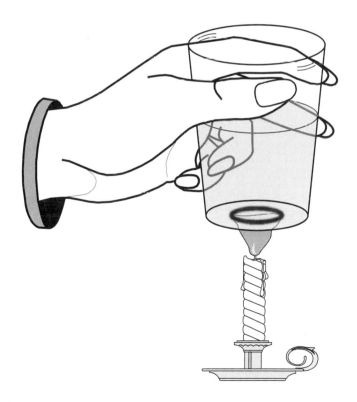

just as water ascends through the narrow openings between the wood fibers of a paper towel. (Remember Experiment 1.3?)

You can see that melted wax flows toward the wick of a burning candle. Just add a few tiny particles of soot to the outer edge of the pool of wax below the flame. You can get the soot by using a toothpick to scrape off some of the black ring from the glass you lowered into the flame. Dip the sooty end of the toothpick into the outer edge of the melted wax. Watch the tiny black specks, carried by the flowing wax, move toward the wick.

What would happen if there were no tiny spaces inside the wick? Would the candle still burn?

To find out, use a pin to make a small hole in the side of a candle. Break a wooden toothpick in half and insert it into the hole as shown in Figure 15. Light the toothpick to see if it will serve as a wick.

Can toothpicks be used as wicks?

Here is yet another way to show that liquid wax ascends the tiny spaces within the wick of a burning candle. With an eyedropper, place one or two drops of water near the edge of the pool of liquid wax at the base of the candle flame. Because water is heavier (for the same volume) than wax, the water will flow under

FIGURE 15

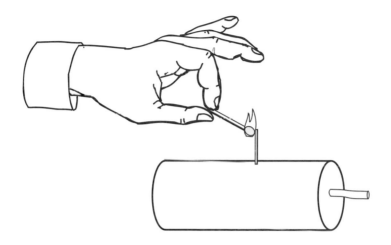

the hot wax. What do you think will happen as the water reaches and ascends the wick? Watch and see if you are right.

The wax that nourishes the flame cannot move up the wick unless it is liquid. Where do you think the heat needed to melt the wax comes from?

What will happen if you reflect the heat away from the candle flame? You can find out by sliding a slit piece of aluminum foil (a good heat reflector) around the wick just below the flame but above the pool of wax as shown in Figure 16.

Why do you think the flame goes out after a minute or so?

FIGURE 16

A prediction: Will a thick candle always produce a bigger flame than a thin candle? Test your prediction with candles of various sizes. What do you find? What does determine the size of the candle's flame?

Experiment 4.6

CANDLES AND AIR

To do this experiment you will need:

- ✔ an ADULT
- ✔ matches
- ✔ birthday candle
- ✔ tin-can lid
- ✔ pint glass jar

Would a giant candle burn for days in a room so well sealed that no fresh air could enter? It is difficult to build such a room, but you can see what happens in a small sealed "room."

This is another experiment that requires matches and flames, so **ask a parent or other adult to work with you**.

Light a birthday candle. When it is burning well, tip the candle so that a few drops of melted wax fall on a tin-can lid. Put the base of the candle into the melted wax to fasten it to the metal lid.

Turn a pint glass jar upside down and lower it over the burning candle. (See Figure 17.) How long does the candle burn in this pint-sized room? How long do you think the candle

FIGURE 17

pint glass jar

wax

will burn in a quart-sized room? How long will
it burn if you cover it with a gallon jar?

OXYGEN AND A BURNING CANDLE

To do this experiment you will need:

- ✔ steel wool
- ✔ jar
- ✔ white vinegar
- ✔ water
- ✔ sink
- ✔ tall, thin jars, such as olive jars
- ✔ pan
- ✔ rubber band, tape, or marking pen
- ✔ clay
- ✔ birthday candles
- ✔ an ADULT
- ✔ matches
- ✔ soap or detergent

How much of the oxygen in a closed space does a candle use up before it goes out? This experiment will help you find out, but again **you will need an adult to help as you light matches and use flames**.

To do this experiment you will need one or more tall, thin jars like the kind olives come in. You will also need birthday candles, steel wool, clay, water, matches, and vinegar. Most steel wool comes in packages that hold six large rolls. From one roll you can make about a dozen small, loosely-rolled balls of steel wool for this experiment. "Pickle" the steel-wool balls by soaking them overnight in a jar that contains one part white vinegar and two parts water. The pickling process will remove the protective coating on the steel.

Remove one of the pickled steel-wool balls from the jar and shake it dry over the sink. Push the steel-wool ball to the bottom of a tall, narrow jar. Turn the jar upside down and place it in a pan of shallow water as shown in Figure 18a. Iron in the steel combines with the

FIGURE 18

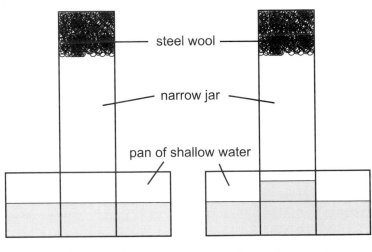

a) before reaction b) after iron reacts with oxygen in air

oxygen above the water in the jar. You will see the water level rise in the jar. The water replaces the oxygen that has combined with the iron to form iron oxide (rust). (See Figure 18b.) After twenty-four hours, mark the water level in the jar. What fraction of the air in the jar was oxygen? (Assume that all the oxygen in the jar combined with the iron.)

Repeat the experiment several times. Are the results the same for each trial?

Use a small piece of clay to support a birthday candle. Place the candle in some shallow water in a container. **Under adult supervision**, light the candle. Then cover it with the tall, narrow jar you used to see how much of the air would react with steel wool. (See Figure 19.) As you can see, water rises up the jar, but did you see bubbles of expanding air emerge from the bottom of the jar?

Does the water rise up in the jar because the burning candle uses up all the oxygen from the air as it burns out or because the cooling air occupies less volume than it did when it was heated by the candle? What fraction of the air in the jar has been replaced by water?

Repeat the experiment several times. Does the water always rise to the same level in the jar?

Put a little soap or detergent in the shallow water and repeat the experiment. Can you see bubbles of gas forming at the mouth of the jar when it is placed over the burning candle? What could explain the presence of these bubbles?

Repeat the experiment, but this time put a ball of steel wool in the bottom of the tall, thin jar. (See Figure 20.) Mark the water level in the jar after the candle goes out and the water stops rising. After twenty-four hours, check the water level in the jar again. Did the candle use up all the oxygen in the jar when it burned? What made the water level rise higher in the jar during the twenty-four-hour period? How does the water level rise during the twenty-four hours after the candle went out compare with the rise when there was only steel wool in the jar?

FIGURE 19

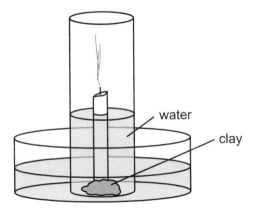

FIGURE 20

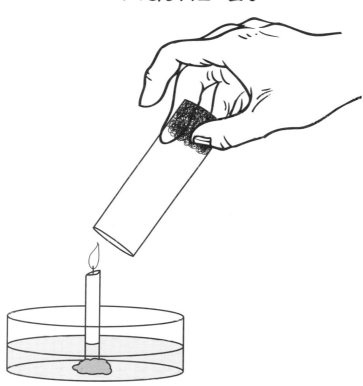

Perhaps the water level will rise in any jar in which a candle has burned. To find out, invert a jar over a burning candle. When the water stops rising, mark its level with a rubber band, tape, or a marking pen, and leave the jar for twenty-four hours. Does the water level change very much?

What fraction of air seems to be oxygen?

What fraction of the oxygen in air is used by a burning candle before it goes out?

Experiment 4.8*

COLORED LIQUIDS THAT SINK OR FLOAT

To do this experiment you will need:

- ✔ kosher salt
- ✔ water
- ✔ 3 containers
- ✔ teaspoon
- ✔ green, red, blue, and yellow food coloring
- ✔ 4 clear pill vials or medicine cups
- ✔ eyedropper
- ✔ balance or scale, optional

Make a saturated salt solution by adding 60 to 70 grams of salt (20 to 25 tsp) to 200 ml (7 fluid oz) of water. Continue to add salt, if necessary, until no more will dissolve. If possible, use kosher salt. Remember that most ordinary table salts have added ingredients that make their solutions cloudy. You will probably need 35 grams (40 to 50 tsp) of the kosher variety to make a saturated solution.

Pour the saturated solution into another container to separate it from any undissolved salt.

Pour *half* of the saturated solution (100 ml, or about 3 1/2 fluid oz) into a second container. Dilute this portion by adding to it an equal volume of water (100 ml, or 3 1/2 fluid oz).

Pour half of this diluted solution into a third container. Dilute this liquid still further by adding an equal volume (100 ml, or 3 1/2 fluid oz) of water.

You now have three solutions: one is saturated; the second has half as much salt per volume of liquid as the first; the third has only one fourth as much salt per volume of liquid as the first.

To identify these different solutions, add a few drops of green food coloring to the first, or saturated, solution. Color the second solution with red food coloring. Make the third, or least concentrated, solution blue.

Obtain four clear pill vials or medicine cups. Put them side by side on the kitchen counter. Fill the first vial about three fourths full with the green (saturated) salt solution. Pour some of the red solution into the second vial; add some blue solution to the third vial. Pour plain water into the fourth vial. If you want a fourth color, add a couple of drops of yellow food coloring to the water.

Use an eyedropper to remove some of the red solution from the second vial. Place the tip

FIGURE 21

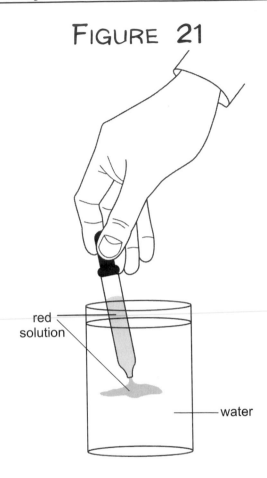

red
solution

water

of the dropper in the middle of the water in the fourth vial. *Gently* squeeze a little of the red solution out into the water, as shown in Figure 21. Does the red liquid sink or rise in the water?

Repeat the experiment in the blue liquid. Does the red liquid rise or sink when it is squeezed gently into the blue solution? What happens when the red liquid flows from the medicine dropper into the green liquid? Does it rise or sink?

What will happen if you gently squeeze a drop of green solution into each of the other three liquids? How about drops of the blue solution in the other liquids? In which liquids does the blue liquid sink? In which one(s) does it rise? Can you predict what will happen if you squeeze a little water from the fourth vial into the other three liquids?

A prediction: Which of these four liquids do you think is the heaviest; that is, which one weighs the most if you weigh equal volumes of all four? If you have a balance or scale (see Experiment 2.4) you can test your predictions by using the same container to weigh equal volumes—say, about 100 ml (3 or 4 fluid oz) of each liquid.

Save your colored liquids for the next experiment.

Experiment 4.9*

COLORED-LIQUID LAYERS

To do this experiment you will need:

✔ transparent plastic straw	✔ apple juice
✔ water	✔ vinegar
✔ glass	✔ salad oil
✔ four colored solutions from Experiment 4.8	✔ syrup
	✔ grape juice
✔ rubbing alcohol	✔ vial or medicine cup
✔ cooking oil	✔ eyedropper
✔ cranberry juice	

A *pipette* can be used to pick up and move liquids. You can make your own pipette from a straw. And with a transparent plastic straw, you can make layers of colored liquids.

Begin by perfecting your technique in lifting liquids. Place a straw in a glass of water. Put your index finger over the upper end of the straw and lift the straw from the water. (See Figure 22.) Air pressure holds the water in the straw. Lift your finger, and the pressure at both ends of the liquid becomes equal. The water flows out of the straw.

FIGURE 22

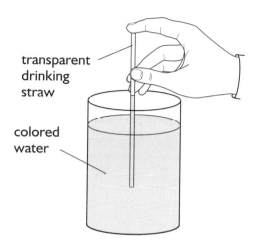

transparent
drinking
straw

colored
water

Once you are good at moving liquids with your see-through straw, you can make a two-layered, colored-liquid "cake" in the straw.

Dip the straw a short way into a vial of the blue liquid you prepared in Experiment 4.8. Put your finger over the straw and lift it out of the liquid. Keeping your finger over the top of the straw, place the straw and the blue liquid within it into the red solution. Push the straw deep enough into the liquid so that the blue liquid in the straw is lower than the surface of the red liquid in the vial. Then release your finger. Red liquid will enter the straw pushing the blue liquid upward until it is even with the surface of the red liquid in the vial.

Now put your finger back on the top of the straw and lift the straw out of the red liquid. Look! You have made a two-layered, colored-liquid "cake"—blue on top of red!

Why can't you make a two-layered cake with the red liquid on top of the blue?

How many two-layered cakes can you make from the four liquids? How many three-layered cakes can you prepare? Can you make a four-layered cake?

Using rubbing alcohol and cooking oil as well as the other four liquids, how many two-, three-, and four-layered cakes can you make? Can you make five-layered cakes? How many? Can you make a six-layered cake? Which liquid is always the top layer? Which liquid is always the bottom layer?

List these six liquids according to their heaviness (weight for the same volume). Put the lightest liquid at the top and the heaviest liquid at the bottom of your list.

Using your method of making liquid layers, see if you can place some of the following liquids in their proper slots on your heaviness list: cranberry juice, apple juice, vinegar, salad oil, syrup, and grape juice.

From what you have learned, make liquid layers in a vial or medicine cup using an eyedropper to move liquids.

A prediction: If you make a two-layered, colored-liquid cake and then turn the straw upside down, will the layers remain separated? What will happen when you turn the straw right side up again?

FURTHER READING

Gardner, Robert. *Science Projects About Physics in the Home.* Springfield, N.J.: Enslow Publishers, Inc., 1999.

Loeschnig, Louis V. *Simple Chemistry Experiments with Everyday Materials.* New York: Sterling Publishing Company, 1995.

Mebane, R. and T. R. Rybolt. *Adventures with Atoms and Molecules, Book V: Chemistry Experiments for Young People.* Springfield, N.J.: Enslow Publishers, Inc., 1995.

Moje, Steven W. *Cool Chemistry: Great Experiments with Simple Stuff.* New York: Sterling Publishing Company, 1999.

Tocci, Salvatore. *How to Do a Science Fair Project.* Revised Edition. Danbury, Conn.: Franklin Watts, 1997.

Internet Addresses

Ask-A-Scientist Archive.
<http://www.newton.dep.anl.gov/archive.htm>.

Internet Public Library. *Science Fair Project Guide.*
<http://www.si.edu/resource/faq/start.htm>.

Rader New Media. *Chem4Kids.com.* "Acids and Bases Are Everywhere." 1998.
<http://chem4kids/reactions/acidbase.html>.

USDA. "Food and Nutrition Science Fair Project Resource List." *General Resources.* May 1996.
<http://www.nal.usda.gov/fnic/pubs/bibs/gen/scifbr.htm>.

INDEX

A
acids, 98–101
air
    and candles, 111–112
    pressure, 76–77
    when heated and cooled,
      74–75
ammonia, 99–100

B
baking, 83–84
bases, 98–101
bending light, 93–94
    to make things disappear,
      93–94
Black, Joseph, 68–70, 72–73
bleach, 87–90
boiling, 72–73
Btu (British thermal unit),
    69–70
buttons, 102–103

C
calories, 68
candle
    and air, 111–112
    burning, 106–110
    leaping flame, 104–105
    and oxygen, 113–117
    wicks, 107–109
capillarity, 17–20
carbon dioxide, 41–46, 74,
    102
    and baking, 83–84
    bubbles, 43–45
    and fire extinguishers,
      41–42
chromatography, 21

colors
    and flowers, 19–20
    liquid, 118–121
    separating, 21–22
convection, 38–40
crystals
    alum, 80–82
    growing, 80–82
    hypo, 78–79

F
flame leaping, 104–105
freezing water, 55–56
    and salt, 57–58

G
gases
    bubbles, 43–45, 102–103
    cooling, 47–48
    in gases, 36–37
    hot and cold, 74
grape juice (unsweetened),
    99–100

I
ice
    floating and sinking,
      61–64
    heat to melt, 67–70
    keeping, 65–66
    lifting without touching,
      58
    melting, 49–54

L
liquids
    climbing, 12–15
    colored, 118–121
    drops, 9–11

layers, 122–125
  in liquids, 35
litmus, 99–100

M
melting, 49–54, 57–58
  factors affecting, 50–53

O
oxygen, 113–117
  fraction in air, 114–117

P
paper towels, 15–17, 20–25
  drying, 15

R
raisins, 103

S
solutes, 29–33
  gases, 36–37
  salt, 31–32

sugar, 30–31, 33
solutions, 29–37, 78–79
  definition, 29
  liquids in liquids, 35
  saturated, 30
  and stirring, 30
  supersaturated, 78–79
  and temperature, 31
solvents, 29, 34
starch, 96–97
  and iodine, 96–97

V
vinegar, 99–100

W
water
  falling, 26–27
  heaping, 7–8
  heat to boil, 72–73
  invisible skin, 28–29